MY FIRST Poem 2016

Poems From Cheshire & Lancashire

Edited By Sarah Washer

First published in Great Britian in 2016 by:

YoungWriters

Coltsfoot Drive
Peterborough
PE2 9BF
Telephone: 01733 890066
Website: www.youngwriters.co.uk

Book Design by Ben Reeves

SB ISBN 978-1-78624-313-3
Printed and bound in the UK by BookPrintingUK
Website: www.bookprintinguk.com
YB0273L

Foreword

Young Writers was established in 1991 with the aim of encouraging writing skills in young people and giving them the opportunity to see their work in print. Poetry is a wonderful way to introduce young children to the idea of rhyme and rhythm and helps learning and development of communication, language and literacy skills.

'My First Poem' was created to introduce nursery and preschool children to this wonderful world of poetry. They were given a template to fill in with their own words, creating a poem that was all about them.

We are proud to present the resulting collection of personal and touching poems in this anthology, which can be treasured for years to come.

Jenni Bannister
Editorial Manager

Contents

Brook Farm Children's Nursery, Barnoldswick

Children R Us Preschool, Preston

Chorley St James Nursery, Chorley

Garstang Preschool & Nursery, Preston

Jeffreys Corner Private Day Nursery, Dukinfield

The Poems

My First Poem

My name is Jake and I go to preschool,
My best friend is Ewan, who is really cool.
I watch Mickey Mouse on TV,
Playing with cars is lots of fun for me.
I just love sausages to eat,
And sometimes chocolate for a treat.
Blue is a colour I like a lot,
My Batman is the best present I ever got.
My favourite person is Mummy, who is a gem,
So this, my first poem, is just for them!

Jake Finney (4)
Acorn Childcare Nursery, Northwich

My First Poem

My name is Alfie and I go to preschool,
My best friend is Shauny, who is really cool.
I watch PAW Patrol on TV,
Playing with sand and water is lots of
fun for me.
I just love Rice Crispies to eat,
And sometimes chocolate for a treat.
Green is a colour I like a lot,
My Peppa Pig is the best present I ever got.
My favourite person is Harvey, who is a gem,
So this, my first poem, is just for them!

Alfie Siddall (3)

Acorn Childcare Nursery, Northwich

My First Poem

My name is Freddie and I go to preschool,
My best friend is Ewan, who is really cool.
I watch Ant Man on TV,
Playing black Spider-Man is lots of fun for me.
I just love sausages to eat,
And sometimes chocolate for a treat.
Blue is a colour I like a lot,
My Ant Man is the best present I ever got.
My favourite person is Mummy, who is a gem,
So this, my first poem, is just for them!

Freddie Lightfoot (3)
Acorn Childcare Nursery, Northwich

My First Poem

My name is Sophia and I go to preschool,
My best friend is Eloise, who is really cool.
I watch Toy Story on TV,
Playing with Jessie is lots of fun for me.
I just love pasta to eat,
And sometimes chocolate for a treat.
Orange is a colour I like a lot,
My Barbie is the best present I ever got.
My favourite person is Barbie, who is a gem,
So this, my first poem, is just for them!

Sophia McCormack (3)
Acorn Childcare Nursery, Northwich

My First Poem

My name is Bluebell and I go to preschool,
My best friend is Skye, who is really cool.
I watch PAW Patrol on TV,
Playing with the tea set is lots of fun for me.
I just love cake to eat,
And sometimes a piece of caterpillar cake
for a treat.
Green is a colour I like a lot,
My Elsa doll is the best present I ever got.
My favourite person is Skye, who is a gem,
So this, my first poem, is just for them!

Bluebell Jones (3)

Acorn Childcare Nursery, Northwich

My First Poem

My name is Eloise and I go to preschool,
My best friend is Grace, who is really cool.
I watch Peppa Pig on TV,
Playing Frozen games is lots of fun for me.
I just love pasta to eat,
And sometimes spaghetti hoops for a treat.
Pink is a colour I like a lot,
My Frozen wand is the best present I ever got.
My favourite people are Mummy and Daddy,
who are gems,
So this, my first poem, is just for them!

Eloise Katie Jones (3)

Acorn Childcare Nursery, Northwich

My First Poem

My name is Benjamin and I go to preschool,
My best friend is Hugo, who is really cool.
I watch Lion King on TV,
Playing with the blue toy is lots of fun for me.
I just love pasta to eat,
And sometimes chocolate ice cream for a treat.
Blue is a colour I like a lot,
My chocolate is the best present I ever got.
My favourite person is Daddy, who is a gem,
So this, my first poem, is just for them!

Benjamin Watts (3)
Acorn Childcare Nursery, Northwich

My First Poem

My name is Jack and I go to preschool,
My best friend is Hugo, who is really cool.
I watch Minions on TV,
Playing with the wheel thing is lots of fun for me.
I just love apples and bananas to eat,
And sometimes chocolate for a treat.
Yellow is a colour I like a lot,
My Mickey Mouse Clubhouse is the best present
I ever got.
My favourite person is Mummy, who is a gem,
So this, my first poem, is just for them!

Jack Thomas Brophy (3)
Acorn Childcare Nursery, Northwich

My First Poem

My name is Joey and I go to preschool,
My best friend is Ewan, who is really cool.
I watch dinosaurs on TV,
Playing with dinosaurs is lots of fun for me.
I just love sausages to eat,
And sometimes sweets for a treat.
Blue is a colour I like a lot,
My dinosaur is the best present I ever got.
My favourite person is Mummy, who is a gem,
So this, my first poem, is just for them!

Joseph Gateley (3)
Acorn Childcare Nursery, Northwich

My First Poem

My name is Hugo and I go to preschool,
My best friend is Skye, who is really cool.
I watch PAW Patrol on TV,
Playing with choo choo trains is lots
of fun for me.
I just love apples to eat,
And sometimes chocolate for a treat.
Black is a colour I like a lot,
My robot is the best present I ever got.
My favourite person is Ewan, who is a gem,
So this, my first poem, is just for them!

Hugo Baird (3)

Acorn Childcare Nursery, Northwich

My First Poem

My name is Ewan and I go to preschool,
My best friend is Joey, who is really cool.
I watch PAW Patrol on TV,
Playing with chainsaws is lots of fun for me.
I just love pasta to eat,
And sometimes chocolate biscuits for a treat.
Black is a colour I like a lot,
My Minion is the best present I ever got.
My favourite person is Shauney, who is a gem,
So this, my first poem, is just for them!

Ewan Scott (4)
Acorn Childcare Nursery, Northwich

My First Poem

My name is Harry and I go to preschool,
My best friend is Mummy, who is really cool.
I watch The Gruffalo on TV,
Playing with animals is lots of fun for me.
I just love chicken to eat,
And sometimes chocolate and sweets
for a treat.
Blue is a colour I like a lot,
My toys (all of them) are the best presents
I ever got.
My favourite person is Mummy, who is a gem,
So this, my first poem, is just for them!

Harry Jarvis (4)

Acorn Childcare Nursery, Northwich

My First Poem

My name is Grace and I go to preschool,
My best friend is Sophia, who is really cool.
I watch Maya the Bee on TV,
Playing with sand is lots of fun for me.
I just love pasta to eat,
And sometimes sweets for a treat.
Pink is a colour I like a lot,
My hairdryer is the best present I ever got.
My favourite person is Mummy, who is a gem,
So this, my first poem, is just for them!

Grace Quinton-Morton (3)
Acorn Childcare Nursery, Northwich

My First Poem

My name is Kian and I go to preschool,
My best friend is my brother, who is really cool.
I watch Tom and Jerry on TV,
Playing with motorbikes is lots of fun for me.
I just love mushrooms to eat,
And sometimes big sweeties for a treat.
Blue is a colour I like a lot,
My electric scooter is the best present I ever got.
My favourite person is Daddy, who is a gem,
So this, my first poem, is just for them!

Kian William Hartt (3)

Acorn Childcare Nursery, Northwich

My First Poem

My name is Josh and I go to preschool,
My best friend is Shauney, who is really cool.
I watch Postman Pat on TV,
Playing with cars is lots of fun for me.
I just love pasta to eat,
And sometimes sweeties for a treat.
Blue is a colour I like a lot,
My pirate costume is the best present I ever got.
My favourite person is Woody, who is a gem,
So this, my first poem, is just for them!

Joshua Allen (3)
Acorn Childcare Nursery, Northwich

My First Poem

My name is Ben and I go to preschool,
My best friend is Mummy, who is really cool.
I watch football on TV,
Playing with toys is lots of fun for me.
I just love crackers to eat,
And sometimes a burger for a treat.
Blue is a colour I like a lot,
My big present is the best present I ever got.
My favourite people are Mummy, Nanna
and Sam, who are gems,
So this, my first poem, is just for them!

Benjamin Williamson (3)
Acorn Childcare Nursery, Northwich

My First Poem

My name is Izzy and I go to preschool,
My best friend is Skye, who is really cool.
I watch Peppa Pig on TV,
Playing with the kitchen is lots of fun for me.
I just love porridge to eat,
And sometimes sweeties for a treat.
Blue is a colour I like a lot,
My tool box is the best present I ever got.
My favourite person is Max, who is a gem,
So this, my first poem, is just for them!

Mike Watson (3)

Acorn Childcare Nursery, Northwich

My First Poem

My name is Skye and I go to preschool,
My best friends are Izzy and Sophia,
who are really cool.
I watch Tiny Pop on TV,
Playing with my Belle Toy is lots of fun for me.
I just love stuffed pasta to eat,
And sometimes cookies for a treat.
Purple is a colour I like a lot,
My Frozen torch is the best present I ever got.
My favourite person is Shaun, who is a gem,
So this, my first poem, is just for them!

Skye Savage (4)
Acorn Childcare Nursery, Northwich

My First Poem

My name is Ethan and I go to preschool,
My best friend is Ewan, who is really cool.
I watch Spidey on TV,
Playing Spider-Man games is lots of fun for me.
I just love sweetcorn to eat,
And sometimes chocolate for a treat.
Red is a colour I like a lot,
My motorbike is the best present I ever got.
My favourite people are Rory and Jessica,
who are gems,
So this, my first poem, is just for them!

Ethan Hayes (4)

Acorn Childcare Nursery, Northwich

My First Poem

My name is Sophia and I go to preschool,
My best friend is Skye, who is really cool.
I watch Team Umizoomi on TV,
Playing princesses is lots of fun for me.
I just love fish fingers to eat,
And sometimes biscuits for a treat.
Pink is a colour I like a lot,
My My Little Pony is the best present
I ever got.
My favourite person is Shaun, who is a gem,
So this, my first poem, is just for them!

Sophia Malley (4)
Acorn Childcare Nursery, Northwich

My First Poem

My name is Holly and I go to preschool,
My best friend is Hugo, who is really cool.
I watch Dora on TV,
Playing with teddies is lots of fun for me.
I just love sausage and mash to eat,
And sometimes lollipops for a treat.
Pink is a colour I like a lot,
My toy cat is the best present I ever got.
My favourite person is Mummy, who is a gem,
So this, my first poem, is just for them!

Holly Marshall (3)

Acorn Childcare Nursery, Northwich

My First Poem

My name is Hannah and I go to preschool,
My best friend is Tom, who is really cool.
I watch Thomas the Tank Engine on TV,
Playing with water is lots of fun for me.
I just love pasta to eat,
And sometimes chocolate for a treat.
White is a colour I like a lot,
My Big Wolf is the best present I ever got.
My favourite person is James, who is a gem,
So this, my first poem, is just for them!

Hannah Laverty (3)

Acorn Childcare Nursery, Northwich

My First Poem

My name is Sam and I go to preschool,
My best friend is Ella, who is really cool.
I watch Octonauts on TV,
Playing and watching TV is lots of fun for me.
I just love peas to eat,
And sometimes pizza for a treat.
Red is a colour I like a lot,
My blue bed is the best present I ever got.
My favourite people are Mummy and Daddy,
who are gems,
So this, my first poem, is just for them!

Samuel Whitton (3)

Acorn Childcare Nursery, Northwich

My First Poem

My name is Harriet and I go to preschool,
My best friend is Izzy, who is really cool.
I watch Frozen on TV,
Playing with sand is lots of fun for me.
I just love sausages to eat,
And sometimes sweets for a treat.
Red is a colour I like a lot,
My lipstick is the best present I ever got.
My favourite person is Mummy, who is a gem,
So this, my first poem, is just for them!

Harriet North (3)
Acorn Childcare Nursery, Northwich

My First Poem

My name is Patrick and I go to preschool,
My best friend is Ewan, who is really cool.
I watch Power Rangers on TV,
Playing Iron Man games is lots of fun for me.
I just love cheese sandwiches to eat,
And sometimes lollipops for a treat.
Green is a colour I like a lot,
My go-kart is the best present I ever got.
My favourite person is Ava, who is a gem,
So this, my first poem, is just for them!

Patrick Rodway (4)
Acorn Childcare Nursery, Northwich

My First Poem

My name is Elliot and I go to preschool,
My best friend is Patrick, who is really cool.
I watch Spider-Man on TV,
Playing on bikes is lots of fun for me.
I just love mash to eat,
And sometimes sweets for a treat.
Red is a colour I like a lot,
My Spider-Man is the best present I ever got.
My favourite person is Tallulah, who is a gem,
So this, my first poem, is just for them!

Elliot Phillips (4)
Acorn Childcare Nursery, Northwich

My First Poem

My name is Jake and I go to preschool,
My best friend is Skye, who is really cool.
I watch Roary the Racing Car on TV,
Playing with diggers is lots of fun for me.
I just love Hula Hoops to eat,
And sometimes sweets for a treat.
Pink is a colour I like a lot,
My red monster truck is the best present
I ever got.
My favourite person is Madison, who is a gem,
So this, my first poem, is just for them!

Jake Hayes (4)
Acorn Childcare Nursery, Northwich

My First Poem

My name is Joey and I go to preschool,
My best friend is Hugo, who is really cool.
I watch Blaze on TV,
Playing Spider-Man games is lots of fun for me.
I just love carrots to eat,
And sometimes marshmallows for a treat.
Red is a colour I like a lot,
My blue Turtle is the best present I ever got.
My favourite person is Daddy, who is a gem,
So this, my first poem, is just for them!

Joseph Leonard Astles (3)

Acorn Childcare Nursery, Northwich

My First Poem

My name is Hafsa and I go to preschool,
My best friend is Muiz, who is really cool.
I watch Thomas the Tank Engine on TV,
Playing with my trains is lots of fun for me.
I just love Idleey to eat,
And sometimes sweets for a treat.
Blue and red are colours I like a lot,
My bike is the best present I ever got.
My favourite person is Daddy, who is a gem,
So this, my first poem, is just for them!

Hafsa Khan (3)
Al-Ikhlaas Nursery, Nelson

My First Poem

My name is Amin Miah and I go to preschool,
My best friend is Maria, my sister, who is really cool.
I watch Paddington Bear on TV,
Playing with Lego is lots of fun for me.
I just love pasta with sauce to eat,
And sometimes sweeties for a treat.
Green is a colour I like a lot,
My art set with crayons is the best present
I ever got.
My favourite person is Maria, my sister, who is a gem,
So this, my first poem, is just for them!

Muhammad Amin Miah (4)
Al-Ikhlaas Nursery, Nelson

My First Poem

My name is Khadijah and I go to preschool,
My best friend is Hannah, who is really cool.
I watch My Little Pony on TV,
Playing with my dolly is lots of fun for me.
I just love rice and pasta to eat,
And sometimes chocolate for a treat.
Gold is a colour I like a lot,
My Play-Doh kit is the best present I ever got.
My favourite person is my daddy, who is a gem,
So this, my first poem, is just for them!

Khadijah Noor Hussain (4)

Al-Ikhlaas Nursery, Nelson

My First Poem

My name is Safa and I go to preschool,
My best friend is Saaliha, who is really cool.
I watch Charlie and Lola on TV,
Playing with dolls is lots of fun for me.
I just love chips to eat,
And sometimes jelly and custard for a treat.
Purple is a colour I like a lot,
My Frozen doll is the best present I ever got.
My favourite person is Mum, who is a gem,
So this, my first poem, is just for them!

Safa Ansir (4)
Al-Ikhlaas Nursery, Nelson

My First Poem

My name is Uwais and I go to preschool,
My best friend is Bilaal, who is really cool.
I watch the film Cars on TV,
Playing Minecraft is lots of fun for me.
I just love pizza with garlic sauce to eat,
And sometimes chocolate for a treat.
Orange is a colour I like a lot,
My Lamborghini Gallardo is the best present
I ever got.
My favourite person is my dad, Nasir, who is a gem,
So this, my first poem, is just for them!

Uwais Nasar (4)
Al-Ikhlaas Nursery, Nelson

My First Poem

My name is Hannah and I go to preschool,
My best friend is Aaminah Layla, who is really cool.
I watch Horrid Henry on TV,
Playing on my bike is lots of fun for me.
I just love fish to eat,
And sometimes an ice cream for a treat.
Blue is a colour I like a lot,
My Lego is the best present I ever got.
My favourite person is my grandma, who is a gem,
So this, my first poem, is just for them!

Hannah Majid (4)
Al-Ikhlaas Nursery, Nelson

My First Poem

My name is Ibrahim and I go to preschool,
My best friend is Issa, who is really cool.
I watch Spider-Man on TV,
Playing with my Hulk is lots of fun for me.
I just love pizza and chips to eat,
And sometimes a cola lolly for a treat.
Blue is a colour I like a lot,
My Batman is the best present I ever got.
My favourite person is my dad, who is a gem,
So this, my first poem, is just for them!

Ibrahim Ali (3)
Al-Ikhlaas Nursery, Nelson

My First Poem

My name is Adam and I go to preschool,
My best friend is Saara, who is really cool.
I watch Roary the Racing Car on TV,
Playing with Lego is lots of fun for me.
I just love chapatis and curry to eat,
And sometimes strawberry ice cream for
a treat.
Red is a colour I like a lot,
My Roary the Racing Car is the best present
I ever got.
My favourite person is my brother, Musa,
who is a gem,
So this, my first poem, is just for them!

Adam Rana (3)
Al-Ikhlaas Nursery, Nelson

My First Poem

My name is Imaan and I go to preschool,
My best friend is Umme Ammarah, who is really cool.
I watch Cinderella on TV,
Playing with Play-Doh is lots of fun for me.
I just love fish and chips to eat,
And sometimes a chocolate for a treat.
Pink is a colour I like a lot,
My Barbie is the best present I ever got.
My favourite person is my mummy, who is a gem,
So this, my first poem, is just for them!

Imaan Ijaz (4)

Al-Ikhlaas Nursery, Nelson

My First Poem

My name is Saara and I go to preschool,
My best friend is Safa, who is really cool.
I watch Minnie Mouse on TV,
Playing with my dolls is lots of fun for me.
I just love pizza to eat,
And sometimes Starburst sweets for a treat.
Pink is a colour I like a lot,
My trip to Disneyland is the best present
I ever got.
My favourite person is Khadijah, my sister,
who is a gem,
So this, my first poem, is just for them!

Saara Ibrahim (3)
Al-Ikhlaas Nursery, Nelson

My First Poem

My name is Umme Ammarah and I go to preschool,
My best friend is my mummy, who is really cool.
I watch Octonauts on TV,
Playing with Pinky, my dolly is lots of fun for me.
I just love lasagne to eat,
And sometimes an ice lolly for a treat.
Pink is a colour I like a lot,
My iPad is the best present I ever got.
My favourite person is my dad, who is a gem,
So this, my first poem, is just for them!

Umme Ammarah Usman (4)
Al-Ikhlaas Nursery, Nelson

My First Poem

My name is Aminah and I go to preschool,
My best friend is Saara, who is really cool.
I watch CBeebies on TV,
Playing with my My Little Pony is lots
of fun for me.
I just love pasta to eat,
And sometimes lollies for a treat.
Pink is a colour I like a lot,
My toy kitchen is the best present I ever got.
My favourite person is my mum, who is a gem,
So this, my first poem, is just for them!

Aminah Hussain (4)
Al-Ikhlaas Nursery, Nelson

My First Poem

My name is Rumaisa and I go to preschool,
My best friend is Khadijah, who is really cool.
I watch Zaki on the iPad on TV,
Playing with my building blocks is lots of
fun for me.
I just love pasta to eat,
And sometimes pizza for a treat.
Pink is a colour I like a lot,
My bead bracelets are the best present
I ever got.
My favourite person is my mum, who is a gem,
So this, my first poem, is just for them!

Rumaisa Saleem (4)
Al-Ikhlaas Nursery, Nelson

My First Poem

My name is Aaminah and I go to preschool,
My best friend is Umme Ammarah, who is really cool.
I watch Mister Maker on TV,
Playing with my colours and drawing is lots of fun for me.
I just love chavel (rice) and curry to eat,
And sometimes Smarties for a treat.
Pink is a colour I like a lot,
My doll from my grandma is the best present I ever got.
My favourite person is my mama, who is a gem,
So this, my first poem, is just for them!

Aaminah Layla Rana (4)
Al-Ikhlaas Nursery, Nelson

My First Poem

My name is Issa and I go to preschool,
My best friend is Ibrahim, who is really cool.
I watch Spider-Man on TV,
Playing with my iPad is lots of fun for me.
I just love chicken to eat,
And sometimes ice cream for a treat.
Blue is a colour I like a lot,
My iPod is the best present I ever got.
My favourite person is my dad, who is a gem,
So this, my first poem, is just for them!

Issa Sajid (4)
Al-Ikhlaas Nursery, Nelson

My First Poem

My name is Beatrice and I go to preschool,
My best friend is Lola, who is really cool.
I watch Ben & Holly on TV,
Playing with puzzles is lots of fun for me.
I just love fish fingers to eat,
And sometimes sweets for a treat.
Pink is a colour I like a lot,
My bike is the best present I ever got.
My favourite person is Florence, who is a gem,
So this, my first poem, is just for them!

Beatrice Bradley (3)
Best Friends Day Nursery, Chester

My First Poem

My name is Freda and I go to preschool,
My best friends are Albie and Dexter,
who are really cool.
I watch Peppa Pig on TV,
Playing push the dice down and move
is lots of fun for me.
I just love carrots to eat,
And sometimes sweets for a treat.
Pink is a colour I like a lot,
My Peppa Pig train is the best present
I ever got.
My favourite person is Mummy, who is a gem,
So this, my first poem, is just for them!

Freda Ward (3)

Best Friends Day Nursery, Chester

My First Poem

My name is Florence and I go to preschool,
My best friend is Freda, who is really cool.
I watch Frozen on TV,
Playing Happy Families is lots of fun for me.
I just love pasta to eat,
And sometimes chocolate biscuits for a treat.
Blue is a colour I like a lot,
My Toy Story is the best present I ever got.
My favourite person is Mummy, who is a gem,
So this, my first poem, is just for them!

Florence Helaina Leadbetter (3)
Best Friends Day Nursery, Chester

My First Poem

My name is Oscar and I go to preschool,
My best friend is Spike, who is really cool.
I watch Splat the Cat on TV,
Playing with cars is lots of fun for me.
I just love fish fingers and chips to eat,
And sometimes cookies for a treat.
Blue is a colour I like a lot,
My toys are the best presents I ever got.
My favourite person is TJ, who is a gem,
So this, my first poem, is just for them!

Oscar Lewis Briggs (4)

Best Friends Day Nursery, Chester

My First Poem

My name is Kornelia and I go to preschool,
My best friend is Minnie, who is really cool.
I watch Elsa and Minions on TV,
Playing with toys is lots of fun for me.
I just love apples and pears to eat,
And sometimes an Elsa egg for a treat.
Purple is a colour I like a lot,
My Minion is the best present I ever got.
My favourite person is Daddy, who is a gem,
So this, my first poem, is just for them!

Kornelia Maya Zygmuntowicz (3)
Bright Futures Nursery, Clitheroe

My First Poem

My name is Jack and I go to preschool,
My best friends are Hollie and Sofia,
who are really cool.
I watch PAW Patrol on TV,
Playing with my big helicopter is lots of
fun for me.
I just love an egg to eat,
And sometimes sweeties for a treat.
Orange is a colour I like a lot,
My big helicopter is the best present I ever got.
My favourite person is Daddy, who is a gem,
So this, my first poem, is just for them!

Jack William Taylor Brierley (3)
Bright Futures Nursery, Clitheroe

My First Poem

My name is Sophie and I go to preschool,
My best friend is Jess, who is really cool.
I watch Mr Bean on TV,
Playing with the Disney castle is lots of fun for me.
I just love beans on toast to eat,
And sometimes a chocolate Milky Way for a treat.
Pink is a colour I like a lot,
My quad bike is the best present I ever got.
My favourite person is Jess, who is a gem,
So this, my first poem, is just for them!

Sophie Holt (3)
Bright Futures Nursery, Clitheroe

My First Poem

My name is Daisy and I go to preschool,
My best friend is Gary my dog, who is really cool.
I watch Scooby-Doo on TV,
Playing Peppa Pig games is lots of fun for me.
I just love fish fingers to eat,
And sometimes chocolate for a treat.
Pink is a colour I like a lot,
My Barbies are the best present I ever got.
My favourite people are Mummy and Daddy,
who are gems,
So this, my first poem, is just for them!

Daisy Fox (3)
Bright Futures Nursery, Clitheroe

My First Poem

My name is Ethan and I go to preschool,
My best friend is Daddy, who is really cool.
I watch PAW Patrol on TV,
Playing Thomas games is lots of fun for me.
I just love sausages, beans, toast and
egg to eat,
And sometimes everything for a treat.
Orange is a colour I like a lot,
My big helicopter is the best present I ever got.
My favourite person is Jenna, who is a gem,
So this, my first poem, is just for them!

Ethan Bank (3)
Bright Futures Nursery, Clitheroe

My First Poem

My name is Isaac and I go to preschool,
My best friends are rabbits and Abygail,
who are really cool.
I watch witchy witches on TV,
Playing with Lego is lots of fun for me.
I just love pancakes to eat,
And sometimes snot sweeties for a treat.
Yellow and green are colours I like a lot,
My fish and Superman are the best presents
I ever got.
My favourite people are Owen and Ashar,
who are gems,
So this, my first poem, is just for them!

Isaac Ridgway (4)
Bright Futures Nursery, Clitheroe

My First Poem

My name is Lily and I go to preschool,
My best friend is Minnie, who is really cool.
I watch Cars on TV,
Playing with Barbies is lots of fun for me.
I just love pasta to eat,
And sometimes worms for a treat.
Pink and black are colours I like a lot,
My dinosaurs are the best present I ever got.
My favourite person is Sofia, who is a gem,
So this, my first poem, is just for them!

Lily Burn (3)

Bright Futures Nursery, Clitheroe

My First Poem

My name is Jessica and I go to preschool,
My best friend is Sophie, who is really cool.
I watch Mr Bean on TV,
Playing on my scooter because it lights up is
lots of fun for me.
I just love tuna to eat,
And sometimes jelly babies from Grandad
for a treat.
Blue is a colour I like a lot,
My scooter that lights up is the best present
I ever got.
My favourite person is Sophie, who is a gem,
So this, my first poem, is just for them!

Jessica Holt (3)
Bright Futures Nursery, Clitheroe

My First Poem

My name is Alice and I go to preschool,
My best friend is Oliver, who is really cool.
I watch Frozen and Peppa Pig on TV,
Playing at home with James' toys is lots of
fun for me.
I just love spaghetti Bolognese to eat,
And sometimes lollipops for a treat.
Yellow is a colour I like a lot,
My cupcake bike is the best present I ever got.
My favourite person is James, who is a gem,
So this, my first poem, is just for them!

Alice Mary Cookson (3)
Bright Futures Nursery, Clitheroe

My First Poem

My name is Jessica and I go to preschool,
My best friend is James, who is really cool.
I watch PAW Patrol on TV,
Playing football is lots of fun for me.
I just love fish fingers to eat,
And sometimes chocolate for a treat.
Pink is a colour I like a lot,
My doll's house is the best present I ever got.
My favourite person is Daddy, who is a gem,
So this, my first poem, is just for them!

Jessica Milly Hudson (4)
Brook Farm Children's Nursery, Barnoldswick

My First Poem

My name is Elliott and I go to preschool,
My best friend is Samuel, who is really cool.
I watch Team Umizoomi on TV,
Playing with my Zurg is lots of fun for me.
I just love cheese on toast to eat,
And sometimes a chocolate muffin for a treat.
Blue is a colour I like a lot,
My kitchen is the best present I ever got.
My favourite person is Mummy, who is a gem,
So this, my first poem, is just for them!

Elliott Allan Hargreaves (4)
Brook Farm Children's Nursery, Barnoldswick

My First Poem

My name is Wren and I go to preschool,
My best friend is Penny, who is really cool.
I watch Octonauts on TV,
Playing on my bike and roller skates is lots of fun for me.
I just love spaghetti Bolognese to eat,
And sometimes chocolate for a treat.
Pink is a colour I like a lot,
My princess castle is the best present I ever got.
My favourite person is Penny, who is a gem,
So this, my first poem, is just for them!

Wren Elizabeth Atkinson (3)
Children R Us Preschool, Preston

My First Poem

My name is Kia-Ann and I go to preschool,
My best friends are Mummy, Daddy, Karis and my family, who are really cool.
I watch Topsy and Tim, Horrid Henry, Scary Shrek, Alvin and Chipmunks
and Frozen on TV,
Playing with toys and friends and painting is
lots of fun for me.
I just love chicken, rice, noodles, ketchup and chocolate eggs to eat,
And sometimes McDonald's, lollipops and ice cream for a treat.
Red, pink, purple and rainbow are colours
I like a lot,
My whiteboard easel and play kitchen are the
best presents I ever got.
My favourite person is Karis, who is a gem,
So this, my first poem, is just for them!

Kia-Ann Brade Aston (3)
Children R Us Preschool, Preston

My First Poem

My name is Williana and I go to preschool,
My best friend is Penny, who is really cool.
I watch Peppa Pig on TV,
Playing on the slide is lots of fun for me.
I just love fish and chips to eat,
And sometimes ice cream for a treat.
Pink is a colour I like a lot,
My Elsa doll from Frozen is the best present
I ever got.
My favourite person is Charlie, who is a gem,
So this, my first poem, is just for them!

Williana Carolina Hoyles (4)
Children R Us Preschool, Preston

My First Poem

My name is Conor and I go to preschool,
My best friend is my daddy, who is really cool.
I watch PJ Masks, Lego, Nexo Knights and
Ninjago on TV,
Playing with the Batman house and Lego is lots
of fun for me.
I just love grapes, cheese and pancakes to eat,
And sometimes Kinder Surprise eggs for a treat.
Blue is a colour I like a lot,
My Lego Next Knights are the best present I ever got.
My favourite person is my daddy, who is a gem,
So this, my first poem, is just for them!

Conor Derek Riley (3)
Children R Us Preschool, Preston

My First Poem

My name is Edward and I go to preschool,
My best friend is Florence, who is really cool.
I watch Thomas on TV,
Playing with trains is lots of fun for me.
I just love maltbread to eat,
And sometimes lollipops for a treat.
Red is a colour I like a lot,
My Thomas onesie is the best present I ever got.
My favourite person is Mummy, who is a gem,
So this, my first poem, is just for them!

Edward James Cross (2)
Children R Us Preschool, Preston

My First Poem

My name is Josie-Jay and I go to preschool,
My best friend is Connor, who is really cool.
I watch Tinkerbell on TV,
Playing with my Jessie doll is lots of fun for me.
I just love cucumber to eat,
And sometimes chocolate cake for a treat.
Blue is a colour I like a lot,
My Shredder from Turtles is the best present
I ever got.
My favourite person is Mummy, who is a gem,
So this, my first poem, is just for them!

Josie-Jay Youd (3)

Children R Us Preschool, Preston

My First Poem

My name is Reuben and I go to preschool,
My best friend is my daddy, who is really cool.
I watch Fireman Sam on TV,
Playing football is lots of fun for me.
I just love chilli and rice to eat,
And sometimes chocolate for a treat.
Blue is a colour I like a lot,
My bike is the best present I ever got.
My favourite person is my family, who is a gem,
So this, my first poem, is just for them!

Reuben Jeory (2)

Children R Us Preschool, Preston

My First Poem

My name is Naomi and I go to preschool,
My best friend is Pheobe, who is really cool.
I watch Pep on TV,
Playing with Shopkins is lots of fun for me.
I just love beans on toast to eat,
And sometimes chocolate for a treat.
Purple is a colour I like a lot,
My Baby 'wee wee' Born is the best present
I ever got.
My favourite person is Daddy, who is a gem,
So this, my first poem, is just for them!

Naomi Taylor (4)
Children R Us Preschool, Preston

My First Poem

My name is Charlie and I go to preschool,
My best friend is Connor, who is really cool.
I watch Ninja Turtles on TV,
Playing at preschool is lots of fun for me.
I just love stinky chicken to eat,
And sometimes yellow lollipops for a treat.
Green and pink are colours I like a lot,
My unicorn is the best present I ever got.
My favourite person is my brother, Max,
who is a gem,
So this, my first poem, is just for them!

Charlie Howarth (4)
Children R Us Preschool, Preston

My First Poem

My name is Oliver and I go to preschool,
My best friends are Connor and Penny,
who are really cool.
I watch PAW Patrol on TV,
Playing PAW Patrol is lots of fun for me.
I just love broccoli to eat,
And sometimes Kinder eggs for a treat.
Blue is a colour I like a lot,
My PAW Patroller and lookout tower
are the best presents I ever got.
My favourite person is Uncle Stu, who is a gem,
So this, my first poem, is just for them!

Oliver Michael Walmsley (3)
Children R Us Preschool, Preston

My First Poem

My name is Faith and I go to preschool,
My best friend is Annabelle, who is really cool.
I watch My Little Pony on TV,
Playing doggies is lots of fun for me.
I just love chicken nuggets, broccoli, mash and gravy to eat,
And sometimes chocolate for a treat.
Pink is a colour I like a lot,
My big dog teddy is the best present I ever got.
My favourite person is Mummy, who is a gem,
So this, my first poem, is just for them!

Faith Oracz (3)
Children R Us Preschool, Preston

My First Poem

My name is Imogen-Willow and I go to preschool,
My best friend is Fabian, who is really cool.
I watch My Little Pony on TV,
Playing with my Play-Doh is lots of fun for me.
I just love spaghetti to eat,
And sometimes cupcakes for a treat.
Pink is a colour I like a lot,
My princess dolls are the best present I ever got.
My favourite person is Mummy, who is a gem,
So this, my first poem, is just for them!

Imogen-Willow Myers (3)
Chorley St James Nursery, Chorley

My First Poem

My name is Harley-James and I go to preschool,
My best friend is Millie-Rose, who is really cool.
I watch PAW Patrol on TV,
Playing in water is lots of fun for me.
I just love chicken nuggets to eat,
And sometimes chocolate for a treat.
Yellow is a colour I like a lot,
My iPad is the best present I ever got.
My favourite person is Mummy, who is a gem,
So this, my first poem, is just for them!

Harley-James Cottom (3)
Chorley St James Nursery, Chorley

My First Poem

My name is Seth and I go to preschool,
My best friend is Sophie, who is really cool.
I watch Mike the Knight on TV,
Playing with Play-Doh is lots of fun for me.
I just love Weetabix to eat,
And sometimes ice cream for a treat.
Blue and red are colours I like a lot,
My dino charger is the best present I ever got.
My favourite person is Zoey, who is a gem,
So this, my first poem, is just for them!

Seth Hart (3)

Chorley St James Nursery, Chorley

My First Poem

My name is Lily and I go to preschool,
My best friend is Leighton, who is really cool.
I watch Mini Monsters on TV,
Playing on my pad is lots of fun for me.
I just love ice cream to eat,
And sometimes chocolate pudding for a treat.
Red is a colour I like a lot,
My StarLily unicorn is the best present I ever got.
My favourite person is my mummy, who is a gem,
So this, my first poem, is just for them!

Lily Howarth (4)
Chorley St James Nursery, Chorley

My First Poem

My name is Lydia and I go to preschool,
My best friend is Auntie Leanne, who is really cool.
I watch movies on TV,
Playing hide-and-seek with my Aunties is lots of fun for me.
I just love blueberries and strawberries to eat,
And sometimes ice cream and cheeseburgers for a treat.
Purple is a colour I like a lot,
My Tigger is the best present I ever got.
My favourite person is Mummy, who is a gem,
So this, my first poem, is just for them!

Lydia May Fullwood Chalkley (4)
Chorley St James Nursery, Chorley

My First Poem

My name is Logan and I go to preschool,
My best friend is my nanny, who is really cool.
I watch Ben & Holly's Little Kingdom on TV,
Playing with my football and Daddy is lots of fun for me.
I just love chocolate and ice cream after pizza to eat,
And sometimes KFC or McDonald's for a treat.
Blue is a colour I like a lot,
My electric motorbike is the best present I ever got.
My favourite person is my mummy, who is a gem,
So this, my first poem, is just for them!

Logan Prescott (3)
Chorley St James Nursery, Chorley

My First Poem

My name is Francis and I go to preschool,
My best friend is Tyler, who is really cool.
I watch Kung Fu Panda on TV,
Playing with helicopters is lots of fun for me.
I just love Star Wars cereal to eat,
And sometimes popcorn chicken for a treat.
Blue is a colour I like a lot,
My giant helicopter is the best present I ever got.
My favourite person is Daddy, who is a gem,
So this, my first poem, is just for them!

Francis Riley (4)

Chorley St James Nursery, Chorley

My First Poem

My name is Noah and I go to preschool,
My best friend is Aaron, who is really cool.
I watch Spider-Man on TV,
Playing with my diggers is lots of fun for me.
I just love lasagne to eat,
And sometimes lollipops for a treat.
Orange is a colour I like a lot,
My Nerf gun is the best present I ever got.
My favourite person is Joel, who is a gem,
So this, my first poem, is just for them!

Noah Dyer (4)
Garstang Preschool & Nursery, Preston

My First Poem

My name is Holly and I go to preschool,
My best friend is Joshua, who is really cool.
I watch Frozen on TV,
Playing on my bike is lots of fun for me.
I just love pasta to eat,
And sometimes sweeties for a treat.
Pink is a colour I like a lot,
My baby is the best present I ever got.
My favourite people are Mummy and Daddy,
who are gems,
So this, my first poem, is just for them!

Holly Baker (4)

Garstang Preschool & Nursery, Preston

My First Poem

My name is Isla and I go to preschool,
My best friend is Tabitha, who is really cool.
I watch Peppa Pig at Nanna's on TV,
Playing with my doll's house is lots of fun for me.
I just love tomato soup to eat,
And sometimes chocolate for a treat.
Pink is a colour I like a lot,
My princess bicycle is the best present I ever got.
My favourite people are Daddy, Mummy and
Pippa, who are gems,
So this, my first poem, is just for them!

Isla Rowlandson (3)
Garstang Preschool & Nursery, Preston

My First Poem

My name is Maisy and I go to preschool,
My best friend is Tabitha who is really cool.
I watch Ben & Holly on TV,
Playing with babies is lots of fun for me.
I just love sausages to eat,
And sometimes chocolate for a treat.
Pink is a colour I like a lot,
My mermaid is the best present I ever got.
My favourite person is Mummy, who is a gem,
So this, my first poem, is just for them!

Maisy Wallbank (4)

Garstang Preschool & Nursery, Preston

My First Poem

My name is Olivia and I go to preschool,
My best friend is Amelia, who is really cool.
I watch Peter Rabbit and Bing on TV,
Playing on my scooter is lots of fun for me.
I just love beans and cheese on toast to eat,
And sometimes biscuits for a treat.
Blue is a colour I like a lot,
My Aquabeads are the best present I ever got.
My favourite people are Mummy, Daddy and Sophia, who are gems,
So this, my first poem, is just for them!

Olivia Assalone (4)
Garstang Preschool & Nursery, Preston

My First Poem

My name is Amelia and I go to preschool,
My best friend is Mia, who is really cool.
I watch Peppa Pig on TV,
Playing on my bike is lots of fun for me.
I just love tuna pasta to eat,
And sometimes Maltesers for a treat.
Purple is a colour I like a lot,
My monster dominoes is the best present
I ever got.
My favourite person is Mummy, who is a gem,
So this, my first poem, is just for them!

Amelia Hooson (4)
Garstang Preschool & Nursery, Preston

My First Poem

My name is Finley and I go to preschool,
My best friend is Harry, who is really cool.
I watch Planes on TV,
Playing on my scooter is lots of fun for me.
I just love pizza to eat,
And sometimes sweeties for a treat.
Red is a colour I like a lot,
My cars are the best present I ever got.
My favourite person is Nana, who is a gem,
So this, my first poem, is just for them!

Finley Tolmie (4)
Garstang Preschool & Nursery, Preston

My First Poem

My name is Mia and I go to preschool,
My best friend is Tabitha, who is really cool.
I watch Frozen on TV,
Playing on my bike is lots of fun for me.
I just love chips to eat,
And sometimes chocolate for a treat.
Brown is a colour I like a lot,
My Peppa Pig phone is the best present
I ever got.
My favourite person is Mummy, who is a gem,
So this, my first poem, is just for them!

Mia Simpson (4)
Garstang Preschool & Nursery, Preston

My First Poem

My name is Maria and I go to preschool,
My best friend is Mia, who is really cool.
I watch Frozen on TV,
Playing with my dollies is lots of fun for me.
I just love cheese toasties to eat,
And sometimes lollipops for a treat.
Purple is a colour I like a lot,
My cake stand and cake are the best presents
I ever got.
My favourite person is Mummy, who is a gem,
So this, my first poem, is just for them!

Maria Thompson (4)

Garstang Preschool & Nursery, Preston

My First Poem

My name is Cruz and I go to preschool,
My best friend is Harry, who is really cool.
I watch Peppa Pig on TV,
Playing with my football is lots of fun for me.
I just love pasta to eat,
And sometimes ice cream for a treat.
Green is a colour I like a lot,
My aeroplane is the best present I ever got.
My favourite person is Daddy, who is a gem,
So this, my first poem, is just for them!

Cruz Cubbins (3)

Garstang Preschool & Nursery, Preston

My First Poem

My name is Tilly and I go to preschool,
My best friend is Annabel, who is really cool.
I watch Frozen on TV,
Playing with Barbies is lots of fun for me.
I just love sandwiches to eat,
And sometimes strawberry cake for a treat.
Pink is a colour I like a lot,
My Baby Born is the best present I ever got.
My favourite person is Maisie, who is a gem,
So this, my first poem, is just for them!

Tilly Rose Leatherbarrow (4)
Garstang Preschool & Nursery, Preston

My First Poem

My name is Benjamin and I go to preschool,
My best friend is Jack, who is really cool.
I watch Mr Incredible on TV,
Playing with Superman is lots of fun for me.
I just love pizza to eat,
And sometimes ice cream for a treat.
Blue is a colour I like a lot,
My Captain America is the best present
I ever got.
My favourite person is Alice, who is a gem,
So this, my first poem, is just for them!

Benjamin Bateman (4)

Garstang Preschool & Nursery, Preston

My First Poem

My name is Annabel and I go to preschool,
My best friend is Olivia, my big sister,
who is really cool.
I watch Frozen on TV,
Playing with Ben and Holly is lots of fun for me.
I just love pasta to eat,
And sometimes sweets for a treat.
Hot pink is a colour I like a lot,
My singing Elsa is the best present I ever got.
My favourite person is Grandma, who is a gem,
So this, my first poem, is just for them!

Annabel Walton (4)
Garstang Preschool & Nursery, Preston

My First Poem

My name is Keira and I go to preschool,
My best friend is Toria, who is really cool.
I watch Peppa Pig on TV,
Playing on my Princess bike is lots of fun for me.
I just love pasta shells to eat,
And sometimes ice lollies for a treat.
Pink is a colour I like a lot,
My Purple Furby is the best present I ever got.
My favourite person is Mummy, who is a gem,
So this, my first poem, is just for them!

Keira Kirkham (4)
Garstang Preschool & Nursery, Preston

My First Poem

My name is James and I go to preschool,
My best friend is Noah, who is really cool.
I watch Teenage Ninja Turtles on TV,
Playing with Optimus Prime is lots of fun for me.
I just love fish fingers, waffles and peas to eat,
And sometimes lollipops for a treat.
Blue is a colour I like a lot,
My Optimus Prime is the best present I ever got.
My favourite person is Mummy, who is a gem,
So this, my first poem, is just for them!

James Vincent Waite (3)
Jeffreys Corner Private Day Nursery, Dukinfield

My First Poem

My name is Abigail and I go to preschool,
My best friend is Cleo, who is really cool.
I watch Mike the Knight on TV,
Playing babies and mummies is lots of
fun for me.
I just love spaghetti to eat,
And sometimes sweeties for a treat.
Pink is a colour I like a lot,
My baby is the best present I ever got.
My favourite person is Mummy, who is a gem,
So this, my first poem, is just for them!

Abigail Taylor (3)
Jeffreys Corner Private Day Nursery, Dukinfield

My First Poem

My name is Boyd and I go to preschool,
My best friend is Eva, who is really cool.
I watch Star Wars on TV,
Playing with Lego is lots of fun for me.
I just love beans to eat,
And sometimes a drink for a treat.
Blue is a colour I like a lot,
My rebels are the best present I ever got.
My favourite person is Giraffe, who is a gem,
So this, my first poem, is just for them!

Boyd Moody (3)

Jeffreys Corner Private Day Nursery, Dukinfield

My First Poem

My name is Lola and I go to preschool,
My best friend is Cleo, who is really cool.
I watch Sarah and Duck on TV,
Playing with cars is lots of fun for me.
I just love sausages to eat,
And sometimes lollies for a treat.
Pink is a colour I like a lot,
My scooter is the best present I ever got.
My favourite person is Mummy, who is a gem,
So this, my first poem, is just for them!

Lola Mae Bell (3)
Jeffreys Corner Private Day Nursery, Dukinfield

My First Poem

My name is Sam and I go to preschool,
My best friend is Boyd, who is really cool.
I watch PAW Patrol on TV,
Playing with my Batman bike is lots of fun for me.
I just love cucumber and peppers to eat,
And sometimes chocolate for a treat.
Blue is a colour I like a lot,
My Batman bike is the best present I ever got.
My favourite person is Daddy, who is a gem,
So this, my first poem, is just for them!

Sam Jack Heyes (4)

Jeffreys Corner Private Day Nursery, Dukinfield

My First Poem

My name is Ethan and I go to preschool,
My best friend is Thomas, who is really cool.
I watch Thomas the Tank Engine on TV,
Playing with building blocks is lots of fun for me.
I just love McDonald's to eat,
And sometimes sweeties for a treat.
Red is a colour I like a lot,
My dice is the best present I ever got.
My favourite person is Thomas, who is a gem,
So this, my first poem, is just for them!

Ethan Taylor (3)
Jeffreys Corner Private Day Nursery, Dukinfield

My First Poem

My name is Belle and I go to preschool,
My best friend is Mum, who is really cool.
I watch Beauty and the Beast on TV,
Playing with my umbrella is lots of fun for me.
I just love spaghetti to eat,
And sometimes sweeties for a treat.
Orange is a colour I like a lot,
My umbrella is the best present I ever got.
My favourite person is Betsy, who is a gem,
So this, my first poem, is just for them!

Belle Sumner (3)
Jeffreys Corner Private Day Nursery, Dukinfield

My First Poem

My name is Ethan and I go to preschool,
My best friend is Noah, who is really cool.
I watch Andy on TV,
Playing with Stickle Bricks is lots of
fun for me.
I just love sandwiches to eat,
And sometimes sweeties for a treat.
Red is a colour I like a lot,
My rubber is the best present I ever got.
My favourite person is Noah, who is a gem,
So this, my first poem, is just for them!

Ethan Norrey (4)
Jeffreys Corner Private Day Nursery, Dukinfield

My First Poem

My name is Tyler and I go to preschool,
My best friend is Jacob, who is really cool.
I watch films on TV,
Playing Domino Topple is lots of fun for me.
I just love everything to eat,
And sometimes popcorn for a treat.
Blue is a colour I like a lot,
My James Bond car is the best present
I ever got.
My favourite person is Jacob, who is a gem,
So this, my first poem, is just for them!

Tyler McGuire (4)
Jeffreys Corner Private Day Nursery, Dukinfield

My First Poem

My name is Jacob and I go to preschool,
My best friend is Brooke, who is really cool.
I watch PAW Patrol on TV,
Playing Hungry Hippos is lots of fun for me.
I just love sausages to eat,
And sometimes chocolate for a treat.
Blue is a colour I like a lot,
My Hungry Hippos game is the best present
I ever got.
My favourite person is Mummy, who is a gem,
So this, my first poem, is just for them!

Jacob Moore (3)
Jeffreys Corner Private Day Nursery, Dukinfield

My First Poem

My name is Lexi and I go to preschool,
My best friend is Katie, who is really cool.
I watch Beauty and the Beast on TV,
Playing with the bricks is lots of fun for me.
I just love chicken and pasta to eat,
And sometimes chocolate for a treat.
Purple is a colour I like a lot,
My teddy bear is the best present I ever got.
My favourite person is Noah, who is a gem,
So this, my first poem, is just for them!

Lexi Coyne (4)

Jeffreys Corner Private Day Nursery, Dukinfield

My First Poem

My name is Hollie and I go to preschool,
My best friend is Cleo, who is really cool.
I watch Peppa Pig on TV,
Playing the guitar is lots of fun for me.
I just love sausages to eat,
And sometimes lollies for a treat.
Purple is a colour I like a lot,
My Peppa Pig is the best present I ever got.
My favourite person is Boyd, who is a gem,
So this, my first poem, is just for them!

Hollie Lowery (3)
Jeffreys Corner Private Day Nursery, Dukinfield

My First Poem

My name is Lexi and I go to preschool,
My best friends are Nanna and Stacey,
who are really cool.
I watch My Little Pony on TV,
Playing My Little Pony is lots of fun for me.
I just love frozen food to eat,
And sometimes cakes for a treat.
Red is a colour I like a lot,
My My Little Pony friends are the best
present I ever got.
My favourite person is Kyle, who is a gem,
So this, my first poem, is just for them!

Lexi Garside (3)
Jeffreys Corner Private Day Nursery, Dukinfield

My First Poem

My name is Sophie and I go to preschool,
My best friend is Jasmin, who is really cool.
I watch Mr Tumble on TV,
Playing with the bricks is lots of fun for me.
I just love bananas to eat,
And sometimes sweeties for a treat.
Pink is a colour I like a lot,
My bike is the best present I ever got.
My favourite person is Ava, who is a gem,
So this, my first poem, is just for them!

Sophie Ribchester (4)
Jeffreys Corner Private Day Nursery, Dukinfield

My First Poem

My name is Cleo and I go to preschool,
My best friend is Grace, who is really cool.
I watch Peppa Pig on TV,
Playing with Peppa Pig cards is lots of fun for me.
I just love sweeties to eat,
And sometimes flapjack for a treat.
Pink is a colour I like a lot,
My Baby Annabell is the best present I ever got.
My favourite person is Mummy, who is a gem,
So this, my first poem, is just for them!

Cleo Kowaltshuk (3)
Jeffreys Corner Private Day Nursery, Dukinfield

My First Poem

My name is Adam and I go to preschool,
My best friend is Sam, who is really cool.
I watch CBeebies on TV,
Playing with my truck is lots of fun for me.
I just love chocolate to eat,
And sometimes sweeties for a treat.
Blue is a colour I like a lot,
My banana present is the best present I ever got.
My favourite person is Mummy, who is a gem,
So this, my first poem, is just for them!

Adam Quinn (4)
Jeffreys Corner Private Day Nursery, Dukinfield

My First Poem

My name is Eddie and I go to preschool,
My best friend is Malakai, who is really cool.
I watch Rescue Bots on TV,
Playing PAW Patrol is lots of fun for me.
I just love pasta to eat,
And sometimes Kinder eggs for a treat.
Blue is a colour I like a lot,
My PAW Patrol lookout is the best present
I ever got.
My favourite person is Mummy, who is a gem,
So this, my first poem, is just for them!

Eddie Stott-Johnson (3)
Jeffreys Corner Private Day Nursery, Dukinfield

My First Poem

My name is Mikey and I go to preschool,
My best friend is Adam, who is really cool.
I watch PAW Patrol on TV,
Playing dinosaurs is lots of fun for me.
I just love pasta to eat,
And sometimes sweets for a treat.
Red is a colour I like a lot,
My PAW Patrol tower is the best present
I ever got.
My favourite person is Adam, who is a gem,
So this, my first poem, is just for them!

Michael Bligh (3)
Jeffreys Corner Private Day Nursery, Dukinfield

My First Poem

My name is Grace and I go to preschool,
My best friend is Nicola, who is really cool.
I watch Frozen on TV,
Playing with Belle is lots of fun for me.
I just love sandwiches to eat,
And sometimes chocolate for a treat.
Pink is a colour I like a lot,
My big Belle is the best present I ever got.
My favourite person is Abigail, who is a gem,
So this, my first poem, is just for them!

Grace Gardiner (3)
Jeffreys Corner Private Day Nursery, Dukinfield

My First Poem

My name is Evie and I go to preschool,
My best friend is Isabelle, who is really cool.
I watch Minions on TV,
Playing with Jessie is lots of fun for me.
I just love chips to eat,
And sometimes sweeties for a treat.
Red is a colour I like a lot,
My bike is the best present I ever got.
My favourite person is Isabelle, who is a gem,
So this, my first poem, is just for them!

Evie Ainsworth (3)
Jeffreys Corner Private Day Nursery, Dukinfield

My First Poem

My name is Millie and I go to preschool,
My best friend is Reuben, who is really cool.
I watch Gem on TV,
Playing with baby dolls is lots of fun for me.
I just love pasta to eat,
And sometimes sweets (Little Stars) for a treat.
Purple, pink and yellow are colours I like a lot,
My Annabell set is the best present I ever got.
My favourite people are Mummy and Daddy,
who are gems,
So this, my first poem, is just for them!

Millie May Johnson-Illidge (4)
Little Weavers Day Nursery, Northwich

My First Poem

My name is Maisie-Dee and I go to preschool,
My best friend is Mummy, who is really cool.
I watch Bob the Builder on TV,
Playing on my tractor is lots of fun for me.
I just love Kinder eggs to eat,
And sometimes tea for a treat.
Blue and pink are colours I like a lot,
My Spider-Man scooter from Grandad
Andy is the best present I ever got.
My favourite person is Daddy, who is a gem,
So this, my first poem, is just for them!

Maisie-Dee Dewison (3)
Little Weavers Day Nursery, Northwich

My First Poem

My name is Oliver and I go to preschool,
My best friend is Emily, who is really cool.
I watch Spider-Man on TV,
Playing with cars is lots of fun for me.
I just love ketchup to eat,
And sometimes chocolate for a treat.
Red and pink are colours I like a lot,
My car is the best present I ever got.
My favourite person is Thomas, who is a gem,
So this, my first poem, is just for them!

Oliver James Stafford (2)
Little Weavers Day Nursery, Northwich

My First Poem

My name is Maisie and I go to preschool,
My best friend is Mummy, who is really cool.
I watch Sooty on TV,
Playing dress-up is lots of fun for me.
I just love spaghetti to eat,
And sometimes crisps for a treat.
Pink is a colour I like a lot,
My scooter is the best present I ever got.
My favourite person is Kelly, who is a gem,
So this, my first poem, is just for them!

Maisie Brooks (3)
Little Weavers Day Nursery, Northwich

My First Poem

My name is Sienna and I go to preschool,
My best friend is Evie, who is really cool.
I watch Charlie and Lola on TV,
Playing the animal game is lots of fun for me.
I just love pizza to eat,
And sometimes raisins for a treat.
Pink is a colour I like a lot,
My dress is the best present I ever got.
My favourite person is Mummy, who is a gem,
So this, my first poem, is just for them!

Sienna Broomfield (2)
Little Weavers Day Nursery, Northwich

My First Poem

My name is Isla and I go to preschool,
My best friend is Emily, who is really cool.
I watch Peppa Pig on TV,
Playing dress-up is lots of fun for me.
I just love Bolognese to eat,
And sometimes sweeties for a treat.
Pink is a colour I like a lot,
My Elsa dress is the best present I ever got.
My favourite person is Joel, who is a gem,
So this, my first poem, is just for them!

Isla Cammack (4)
Little Weavers Day Nursery, Northwich

My First Poem

My name is Sophie and I go to preschool,
My best friend is Millie, who is really cool.
I watch Numberjacks on TV,
Playing with Weebles is lots of fun for me.
I just love fish fingers to eat,
And sometimes cake for a treat.
Purple and pink are colours I like a lot,
My crayons are the best present I ever got.
My favourite person is Daddy, who is a gem,
So this, my first poem, is just for them!

Sophie Astles (4)
Little Weavers Day Nursery, Northwich

My First Poem

My name is Dominic and I go to preschool,
My best friend is Reuben, who is really cool.
I watch Mario on TV,
Playing with Lego is lots of fun for me.
I just love noodles to eat,
And sometimes sweets for a treat.
Red is a colour I like a lot,
My Mairo figures are the best present I ever got.
My favourite people are Daddy and Mummy,
who are gems,
So this, my first poem, is just for them!

Dominic Dearden-Furmedge (3)
Little Weavers Day Nursery, Northwich

My First Poem

My name is James and I go to preschool,
My best friend is Thomas, who is really cool.
I watch Frozen on TV,
Playing Mario games is lots of fun for me.
I just love berries to eat,
And sometimes doughnuts for a treat.
Orange is a colour I like a lot,
My dinosaurs are the best present I ever got.
My favourite people are Mummy and Daddy,
who are gems,
So this, my first poem, is just for them!

James Hazlehurst (4)
Little Weavers Day Nursery, Northwich

My First Poem

My name is **Ben** and I go to preschool,
My best friend is **Dylan**, who is really cool.
I watch **Cars** on TV,
Playing **games** is lots of fun for me.
I just love **sausages** to eat,
And sometimes **jelly** for a treat.
Blue is a colour I like a lot,
My **bike** is the best present I ever got.
My favourite person is **Mummy**, who is a gem,
So this, my first poem, is just for them!

Ben McWhirk (4)
Little Weavers Day Nursery, Northwich

My First Poem

My name is Dexter and I go to preschool,
My best friend is Freddie, who is really cool.
I watch Spider-Man on TV,
Playing with the pirate ship is lots of
fun for me.
I just love chips to eat,
And sometimes raspberries for a treat.
Orange is a colour I like a lot,
My crane is the best present I ever got.
My favourite person is Mummy, who is a gem,
So this, my first poem, is just for them!

Dexter Williamson-Shields (4)
Lynton Private Day Nursery, Warrington

My Second Poem

My name is Angelina and I go to preschool,
My best friend is Freddie, who is really cool.
I watch Curious George on TV,
Playing on my big tablet is lots of fun for me.
I just love wraps to eat,
And sometimes chocolate for a treat.
Pink is a colour I like a lot,
My tablet is the best present I ever got.
My favourite person is Enzo, who is a gem,
So this, my first poem, is just for them!

Angelina Friscuolo (4)
Lynton Private Day Nursery, Warrington

My First Poem

My name is Daniel and I go to preschool,
My best friend is Angelina, who is really cool.
I watch Octonauts on TV,
Playing Batman and Robin is lots of fun for me.
I just love beans on toast to eat,
And sometimes biscuits for a treat.
Blue is a colour I like a lot,
My Duplo is the best present I ever got.
My favourite person is my Daddy, who is a gem,
So this, my first poem, is just for them!

Daniel Brian Laird (3)
Lynton Private Day Nursery, Warrington

My First Poem

My name is Ava and I go to preschool,
My best friend is Daniel, who is really cool.
I watch PAW Patrol on TV,
Playing with bricks is lots of fun for me.
I just love paté to eat,
And sometimes chocolate bars for a treat.
Pink is a colour I like a lot,
My Elsa doll is the best present I ever got.
My favourite person is Millie, who is a gem,
So this, my first poem, is just for them!

Ava Lamb (3)
Lynton Private Day Nursery, Warrington

My First Poem

My name is Freddie and I go to preschool,
My best friend is Archie, who is really cool.
I watch football on TV,
Playing with the dinosaurs is lots of fun for me.
I just love eggs and beans to eat,
And sometimes a chocolate bar for a treat.
Red is a colour I like a lot,
My PAW Patrol tower is the best present I ever got.
My favourite person is my daddy, who is a gem,
So this, my first poem, is just for them!

Freddie Webber (4)
Lynton Private Day Nursery, Warrington

My First Poem

My name is Lexie and I go to preschool,
My best friend is Poppy, who is really cool.
I watch Peppa Pig on TV,
Playing with Play-Doh is lots of fun for me.
I just love everything to eat,
And sometimes chocolate for a treat.
Pink and purple are colours I like a lot,
My pram and baby doll are the best presents
I ever got.
My favourite people are Mummy and Daddy,
who are gems,
So this, my first poem, is just for them!

Lexie Marsh (3)
Newton Park Preschool, Chester

My First Poem

My name is Kiko and I go to preschool,
My best friend is Mandy, who is really cool.
I watch Mickey Mouse Clubhouse on TV,
Playing outside is lots of fun for me.
I just love cereal to eat,
And sometimes chocolate ice cream for a treat.
Purple is a colour I like a lot,
My Mickey Mouse book is the best present
I ever got.
My favourite person is Nanny, who is a gem,
So this, my first poem, is just for them!

Kiko Atkinson (3)
Newton Park Preschool, Chester

My First Poem

My name is Marco and I go to preschool,
My best friend is Alex, who is really cool.
I watch Toy Story on TV,
Playing tag is lots of fun for me.
I just love lunch to eat,
And sometimes a Cheestring for a treat.
Hazel is a colour I like a lot,
My Lego is the best present I ever got.
My favourite person is Mummy, who is a gem.
So this, my first poem, is just for them!

Marco Stather (3)
Newton Park Preschool, Chester

My First Poem

My name is Noah and I go to preschool,
My best friend is Leah, who is really cool.
I watch PAW Patrol on TV,
Playing with toys is lots of fun for me.
I just love beans on toast to eat,
And sometimes a chocolate brownie for a treat.
Yellow is a colour I like a lot,
My Dusty plane is the best present I ever got.
My favourite person is Mason, who is a gem,
So this, my first poem, is just for them!

Noah King (3)
Newton Park Preschool, Chester

My First Poem

My name is Talisha and I go to preschool,
My best friend is Amelia, who is really cool.
I watch Peppa Pig on TV,
Playing on my bike is lots of fun for me.
I just love doughnuts to eat,
And sometimes sweets for a treat.
Orange is a colour I like a lot,
My Elsa castle and Ice Princess are
the best presents I ever got.
My favourite person is Summer, who is a gem,
So this, my first poem, is just for them!

Talisha Smith (3)
Newton Park Preschool, Chester

My First Poem

My name is Harrison and I go to preschool,
My best friend is Noah, who is really cool.
I watch PJ Masks on TV,
Playing with the Disney Colour Changers
is lots of fun for me.
I just love cheeseburgers to eat,
And sometimes a Freddo choccy frog for a treat.
Green is a colour I like a lot,
My elephant is the best present I ever got.
My favourite person is Nana Mo, who is a gem,
So this, my first poem, is just for them!

Harrison John Minnery (4)
Newton Park Preschool, Chester

My First Poem

My name is Jamie and I go to preschool,
My best friends are Sonny and Tommy,
who are really cool.
I watch Scooby-Doo on TV,
Playing with the Scooby-Doo Mystery
Mansion is lots of fun for me.
I just love blueberries and oranges to eat,
And sometimes Scooby snacks for a treat.
Yellow is a colour I like a lot,
My Scooby-Doo figures are the best present
I ever got.
My favourite person is Lewis, who is a gem,
So this, my first poem, is just for them!

Jamie Farrell (4)
Newton Park Preschool, Chester

My First Poem

My name is Amelia and I go to preschool,
My best friend is Talisha, who is really cool.
I watch Topsy and Tim on TV,
Playing with dollies is lots of fun for me.
I just love pasta to eat,
And sometimes jelly for a treat.
Blue is a colour I like a lot,
My Frozen Anna doll is the best present I ever got.
My favourite person is Aunty Roseanna, who is a gem,
So this, my first poem, is just for them!

Amelia Atkinson (4)
Newton Park Preschool, Chester

My First Poem

My name is Shareen and I go to preschool,
My best friend is Janat, who is really cool.
I watch Mr Bean on TV,
Playing with Play-Doh is lots of fun for me.
I just love pasta to eat,
And sometimes a chocolate egg for a treat.
Blue is a colour I like a lot,
My iPad is the best present I ever got.
My favourite person is my mummy, who is a gem,
So this, my first poem, is just for them!

Shareen Shahanum (3)
Newton Park Preschool, Chester

My First Poem

My name is Isaac and I go to preschool,
My best friend is Noah, who is really cool.
I watch PAW Patrol on TV,
Playing with Lego is lots of fun for me.
I just love jam sandwiches to eat,
And sometimes a Kinder egg for a treat.
Yellow is a colour I like a lot,
My talking Minion is the best present I ever got.
My favourite person is Mummy, who is a gem,
So this, my first poem, is just for them!

Isaac Dean (3)

Newton Park Preschool, Chester

My First Poem

My name is Charlie and I go to preschool,
My best friend is James, who is really cool.
I watch Postman Pat on TV,
Playing with puzzles is lots of fun for me.
I just love pasta to eat,
And sometimes sweets and ice cream
for a treat.
Green is a colour I like a lot,
My car is the best present I ever got.
My favourite person is Mummy, who is a gem,
So this, my first poem, is just for them!

Charlie Fairclough (3)

Parbold Nursery School, Wigan

My First Poem

My name is Archer and I go to preschool,
My best friend is Alanna, who is really cool.
I watch Peppa Pig on TV,
Playing with The Hulk is lots of fun for me.
I just love sandwiches to eat,
And sometimes milk for a treat.
Red is a colour I like a lot,
My dinosaur is the best present I ever got.
My favourite person is Mummy, who is a gem,
So this, my first poem, is just for them!

Archer Wood (3)
Parbold Nursery School, Wigan

My First Poem

My name is Vanessa and I go to preschool,
My best friend is Amelia, who is really cool.
I watch Peppa on TV,
Playing dress-up is lots of fun for me.
I just love yoghurt to eat,
And sometimes cake for a treat.
Red is a colour I like a lot,
My baby is the best present I ever got.
My favourite person is Mummy, who is a gem,
So this, my first poem, is just for them!

Vanessa Drampalou (3)
Parbold Nursery School, Wigan

My First Poem

My name is Alanna and I go to preschool,
My best friend is Archer, who is really cool.
I watch Peppa Pig on TV,
Playing bunny rabbits is lots of fun for me.
I just love chips and pasta to eat,
And sometimes ice cream for a treat.
Pink is a colour I like a lot,
My tractor is the best present I ever got.
My favourite person is Mummy, who is a gem,
So this, my first poem, is just for them!

Alanna Elizabeth Hitchen (4)
Parbold Nursery School, Wigan

My First Poem

My name is Oliver and I go to preschool,
My best friend is Max, who is really cool.
I watch PAW Patrol on TV,
Playing with jigsaws is lots of fun for me.
I just love shepherd's pie to eat,
And sometimes sweets for a treat.
Red is a colour I like a lot,
My scooter is the best present I ever got.
My favourite person is Millie, who is a gem,
So this, my first poem, is just for them!

Oliver Robert John Blake (4)
Parbold Nursery School, Wigan

My First Poem

My name is Evelyn and I go to preschool,
My best friend is Alanna, who is really cool.
I watch Topsy and Tim on TV,
Playing dress-up is lots of fun for me.
I just love beans and sausages to eat,
And sometimes chocolate for a treat.
Black is a colour I like a lot,
My Jessie is the best present I ever got.
My favourite person is Sammy, who is a gem,
So this, my first poem, is just for them!

Evelyn Grace Baxter (4)
Parbold Nursery School, Wigan

My First Poem

My name is Albert and I go to preschool,
My best friend is Oliver, who is really cool.
I watch Peppa Pig on TV,
Playing with jigsaws is lots of fun for me.
I just love yoghurt to eat,
And sometimes crisps for a treat.
Green is a colour I like a lot,
My cars are the best present I ever got.
My favourite person is Nanna, who is a gem,
So this, my first poem, is just for them!

Albert Acland (2)
Parbold Nursery School, Wigan

My First Poem

My name is James and I go to preschool,
My best friend is Lucy, who is really cool.
I watch In the Night Garden on TV,
Playing Pop-Up Pirate is lots of fun for me.
I just love eggs to eat,
And sometimes ice cream for a treat.
Orange is a colour I like a lot,
My car is the best present I ever got.
My favourite person is Betsy, who is a gem,
So this, my first poem, is just for them!

James Righton (4)
Parbold Nursery School, Wigan

My First Poem

My name is Sophia and I go to preschool,
My best friend is Zakariya, who is really cool.
I watch Peppa Pig on TV,
Playing with trains is lots of fun for me.
I just love pizza to eat,
And sometimes sweeties for a treat.
Green is a colour I like a lot,
My yo-yo is the best present I ever got.
My favourite person is Daddy, who is a gem,
So this, my first poem, is just for them!

Sophia Lehner (3)
Pendle View Nursery, Blackburn

My First Poem

My name is Aaminah and I go to preschool,
My best friends are Aysha and Zara,
who are really cool.
I watch My Little Pony on TV,
Playing with my dolls is lots of fun for me.
I just love sausages, potatoes and gravy
to eat,
And sometimes sweets for a treat.
Pink and purple are colours I like a lot,
My Elsa and Anna dolls are the best presents
I ever got.
My favourite person is my sister, who is a gem,
So this, my first poem, is just for them!

Aaminah Amin (4)
Pendle View Nursery, Blackburn

My First Poem

My name is Henry and I go to preschool,
My best friends are everyone, who are really cool.
I watch Ben & Holly on TV,
Playing in my bedroom is lots of fun for me.
I just love a ham sandwich and jam to eat,
And sometimes ice cream and yoghurts
for a treat.
Blue is a colour I like a lot,
My Hulk toy is the best present I ever got.
My favourite people are everyone, who are gems,
So this, my first poem, is just for them!

Henry Adams (4)
Pendle View Nursery, Blackburn

My First Poem

My name is Isabelle and I go to preschool,
My best friends are Sophia and Eva,
who are really cool.
I watch Peppa Pig on TV,
Playing with my magnets is lots of fun for me.
I just love pasta to eat,
And sometimes ice cream for a treat.
Pink is a colour I like a lot,
My My Little Pony Play-Doh is the best present
I ever got.
My favourite person is Mummy, who is a gem,
So this, my first poem, is just for them!

Isabelle Hosgood (3)
Pendle View Nursery, Blackburn

My First Poem

My name is Logan and I go to preschool,
My best friend is Eva, who is really cool.
I watch PAW Patrol on TV,
Playing with my rocket is lots of fun for me.
I just love a chicken burger and chips to eat,
And sometimes fruit for a treat.
Res is a colour I like a lot,
My rocket is the best present I ever got.
My favourite person is Mummy, who is a gem,
So this, my first poem, is just for them!

Logan James Williams (3)
Pendle View Nursery, Blackburn

My First Poem

My name is Joseph and I go to preschool,
My best friend is Freddie, who is really cool.
I watch Milkshake on TV,
Playing superheroes is lots of fun for me.
I just love fish and chips to eat,
And sometimes sweeties for a treat.
Red and black are colours I like a lot,
My Ultraman superhero is the best present
I ever got.
My favourite person is Captain America,
who is a gem,
So this, my first poem, is just for them!

Joseph Caulkin (3)
Pendle View Nursery, Blackburn

My First Poem

My name is Louie and I go to preschool,
My best friend is James, who is really cool.
I watch lots of things on TV,
Playing with Lego at my house is lots of
fun for me.
I just love Weetabix to eat,
And sometimes sweeties for a treat.
Blue is a colour I like a lot,
My Power Ranger is the best present I ever got.
My favourite person is Mummy, who is a gem,
So this, my first poem, is just for them!

Louie Houghton-Riding (4)
Pendle View Nursery, Blackburn

My First Poem

My name is Noah and I go to preschool,
My best friend is Esme, who is really cool.
I watch Mickey Mouse on TV,
Playing Power Ranger games is lots of fun for me.
I just love jacket potatoes to eat,
And sometimes chocolate for a treat.
Blue is a colour I like a lot,
My cupcake maker is the best present I ever got.
My favourite person is Mummy, who is a gem,
So this, my first poem, is just for them!

Noah Soliman (4)

Safehands Nursery, Blackpool

My First Poem

My name is Summer-Leigh and I go to preschool,
My best friend is Tyler, who is really cool.
I watch Peppa Pig on TV,
Playing with my Thomas is lots of fun for me.
I just love sandwiches to eat,
And sometimes biscuits for a treat.
Blue is a colour I like a lot,
My doggy is the best present I ever got.
My favourite person is Mummy, who is a gem,
So this, my first poem, is just for them!

Summer-Leigh Ellis (3)
Safehands Nursery, Blackpool

My First Poem

My name is Jaidan and I go to preschool,
My best friend is Mayson, who is really cool.
I watch Turtles on TV,
Playing Spider-Man games is lots of fun for me.
I just love pizza to eat,
And sometimes ice cream for a treat.
Blue is a colour I like a lot,
My chase game is the best present I ever got.
My favourite person is Mummy, who is a gem,
So this, my first poem, is just for them!

Jaidan Brinkley-Baker (3)
Safehands Nursery, Blackpool

My First Poem

My name is Megan and I go to preschool,
My best friend is Olivia, who is really cool.
I watch CBeebies on TV,
Playing babies is lots of fun for me.
I just love cornflakes to eat,
And sometimes Buttons for a treat.
Pink is a colour I like a lot,
My doll is the best present I ever got.
My favourite person is Daddy, who is a gem,
So this, my first poem, is just for them!

Megan Dale (3)
Safehands Nursery, Blackpool

My First Poem

My name is Olivia and I go to preschool,
My best friend is Abbie, who is really cool.
I watch Peppa Pig on TV,
Playing babies is lots of fun for me.
I just love carrots and potatoes to eat,
And sometimes ice cream for a treat.
Blue is a colour I like a lot,
My baby's bottle is the best present I ever got.
My favourite person is Becka, who is a gem,
So this, my first poem, is just for them!

Olivia Brooke Wilson (4)

Safehands Nursery, Blackpool

My First Poem

My name is Lucas and I go to preschool,
My best friend is Tristan, who is really cool.
I watch Ninja Turtles on TV,
Playing SpongeBob games is lots of fun for me.
I just love chicken dinner to eat,
And sometimes chocolate milkshake for a treat.
Red is a colour I like a lot,
My scooter is the best present I ever got.
My favourite person is Max, who is a gem,
So this, my first poem, is just for them!

Lucas Smith (3)

Safehands Nursery, Blackpool

My First Poem

My name is Junior and I go to preschool,
My best friend is Mayson, who is really cool.
I watch Mickey Mouse on TV,
Playing with cars is lots of fun for me.
I just love sausages to eat,
And sometimes jelly for a treat.
Red is a colour I like a lot,
My jigsaw is the best present I ever got.
My favourite person is Mummy, who is a gem,
So this, my first poem, is just for them!

Junior Snee (4)
Safehands Nursery, Blackpool

My First Poem

My name is Charles and I go to preschool,
My best friend is Oliver, who is really cool.
I watch Peter Rabbit on TV,
Playing with motorbikes is lots of fun for me.
I just love pasta to eat,
And sometimes lollipops for a treat.
Purple is a colour I like a lot,
My quad bike is the best present I ever got.
My favourite person is Mummy, who is a gem,
So this, my first poem, is just for them!

Charles Edward Scambler (3)
Whitechapel Preschool Playgroup, Preston

My First Poem

My name is Olivia and I go to preschool,
My best friend is Annie, who is really cool.
I watch Nemo on TV,
Playing with houses is lots of fun for me.
I just love sandwiches to eat,
And sometimes chocolate for a treat.
Red is a colour I like a lot,
My doll's house is the best present I ever got.
My favourite person is Elsie, who is a gem,
So this, my first poem, is just for them!

Olivia Butler (4)
Whitechapel Preschool Playgroup, Preston

My First Poem

My name is Dexter and I go to preschool,
My best friend is Liam, who is really cool.
I watch Octonauts on TV,
Playing with tractors is lots of fun for me.
I just love toast to eat,
And sometimes chocolate for a treat.
Red is a colour I like a lot,
My quad bike is the best present I ever got.
My favourite person is Daddy, who is a gem,
So this, my first poem, is just for them!

Dexter Carl Fletcher (4)

Whitechapel Preschool Playgroup, Preston

My First Poem

My name is Eva and I go to preschool,
My best friend is Alice, who is really cool.
I watch Cinderella on TV,
Playing princesses is lots of fun for me.
I just love sausages to eat,
And sometimes chocolate for a treat.
Pink is a colour I like a lot,
My glass slippers are the best present
I ever got.
My favourite person is Mummy, who is a gem,
So this, my first poem, is just for them!

Eva English (3)
Whitechapel Preschool Playgroup, Preston

My First Poem

My name is Madelaine and I go to preschool,
My best friend is Daniel, who is really cool.
I watch Peppa Pig on TV,
Playing doctors is lots of fun for me.
I just love apples to eat,
And sometimes sweeties for a treat.
Pink is a colour I like a lot,
My jewellery box is the best present I ever got.
My favourite person is Daddy, who is a gem,
So this, my first poem, is just for them!

Madelaine Peall (3)
Whitechapel Preschool Playgroup, Preston

My First Poem

My name is Anna and I go to preschool,
My best friend is Penelope, who is really cool.
I watch Peppa Pig on TV,
Playing in the kitchen is lots of fun for me.
I just love bananas to eat,
And sometimes chocolate for a treat.
Red is a colour I like a lot,
My Peppa Pig knitting set is the best
present I ever got.
My favourite person is Mummy, who is a gem,
So this, my first poem, is just for them!

Anna Coupe-Smith (4)
Whitechapel Preschool Playgroup, Preston

My First Poem

My name is Maisey and I go to preschool,
My best friend is Isla, who is really cool.
I watch Ninja Turtles on TV,
Playing with dragons and castles is lots of fun for me.
I just love chocolate eggs to eat,
And sometimes go swimming for a treat.
Blue is a colour I like a lot,
My dragons are the best present I ever got.
My favourite person is Mummy, who is a gem,
So this, my first poem, is just for them!

Maisey Openshaw (3)

Whitechapel Preschool Playgroup, Preston

My First Poem

My name is Oliver and I go to preschool,
My best friend is Dexter, who is really cool.
I watch Ben & Holly on TV,
Playing with the blocks is lots of fun for me.
I just love pasta parcels to eat,
And sometimes chocolate for a treat.
Blue is a colour I like a lot,
My dinosaur racing car track is the best
present I ever got.
My favourite person is Sam, who is a gem,
So this, my first poem, is just for them!

Oliver Robinson (4)

Whitechapel Preschool Playgroup, Preston

My First Poem

My name is Jack and I go to preschool,
My best friend is Olivia, who is really cool.
I watch Tractor Ted on TV,
Playing farms is lots of fun for me.
I just love beans on toast to eat,
And sometimes sweets for a treat.
Green is a colour I like a lot,
My toy gun is the best present I ever got.
My favourite person is Mummy, who is a gem,
So this, my first poem, is just for them!

Jack Lancashire (4)
Whitechapel Preschool Playgroup, Preston

My First Poem

My name is Robyn and I go to preschool,
My best friend is Olivia, who is really cool.
I watch CBeebies on TV,
Playing mums and dads is lots of fun for me.
I just love rice and beans to eat,
And sometimes sweets and chocolate for a treat.
Pink and blue are colours I like a lot,
My dummy for my dolls is the best present
I ever got.
My favourite person is Mummy, who is a gem,
So this, my first poem, is just for them!

Robyn Hall (3)
Whitechapel Preschool Playgroup, Preston

My First Poem

My name is Alice and I go to preschool,
My best friend is Oliver, who is really cool.
I watch Ladybug & Cat Noir on TV,
Playing with ponies is lots of fun for me.
I just love pasta to eat,
And sometimes lollipops for a treat.
Pink is a colour I like a lot,
My My Little Pony is the best present I ever got.
My favourite person is Martha, who is a gem,
So this, my first poem, is just for them!

Alice Eastham (4)

Whitechapel Preschool Playgroup, Preston

My First Poem

We hope you have enjoyed reading this book - and that you will continue to enjoy it in the coming years.

If you're a young writer who enjoys reading and creative writing, or the parent of an enthusiastic poet or story writer, do visit our websites, www.myfirstpoem.com and www.youngwriters.co.uk. Here you will find free competitions, workshops and games, as well as recommended reads, a poetry glossary and our blog.

If you would like to order further copies of this book, or any of our other titles, then please give us a call or visit www.myfirstpoem.com.

My First Poem
Remus House
Coltsfoot Drive
Peterborough
PE2 9BF

Tel: 01733 898110
info@myfirstpoem.com